Giftbooks in this series by Helen Exley:

Words on Hope   Words on Joy
Words on Courage   Words on Kindness
Words of Wisdom   Words on Love and Caring

Published simultaneously in 1997 by Exley Publications in
Great Britain, and Exley Giftbooks in the USA.

12 11 10 9 8 7 6 5 4 3 2

Edited and pictures selected by Helen Exley
ISBN 1-85015-924-6

Picture research by Image Select International.
Typeset by Delta, Watford.
Printed in China.

Exley Publications Ltd, 16 Chalk Hill, Watford,
Herts WD1 4BN, UK.
Exley Publications LLC, 232 Madison Avenue,
Suite 1206, NY 10016, USA.

Words on Love
& Caring

A HELEN EXLEY
GIFTBOOK

EXLEY
NEW YORK • WATFORD, UK

The more we can love
ourselves and attend to all of
life around us with a loving,
open and connected heart...
the more we can be in a
beautiful place.

BROOKE MEDICINE EAGLE

You live
that you may
learn to love, you love
that you may
learn to live.
No other
lesson is
required of you.

MIRDAD

*L*ove alone is
capable of uniting
living beings
in such a way
as to complete
and fulfil them,
for it alone
takes them
and joins them
by what is deepest
in themselves.

PIERRE
TEILHARD
DE CHARDIN
(1881-1955)

It is love that fashions us into the fullness of our being – not our looks, not our work, not our wants, not our achievements, not our parents, not our status, not our dreams. These are all the fodder and the filler, the navigating fuels of our lives; but it is love: who we love, how we love, why we love and that we love which ultimately shapes us.

DAPHNE ROSE KINGMA

*S*ome day,
after we have mastered
the winds, the waves,
the tides and gravity
we shall harness the energies
of love.
Then, for the second time
in the history of the world,
man will have discovered
fire.

PIERRE TEILHARD
DE CHARDIN
(1881-1955)

He alone is great
who turns the voice
of the wind
into a song
made sweeter
by his own
loving.

KAHLIL
GIBRAN
(1883-1931)

[Infinite Love]
is a weapon
of matchless potency.
It is the "summum bonum"
of Life.
It is an attribute of
the brave, in fact it
is their all.
It does not come within
the reach of the coward.
It is no wooden or lifeless dogma
but a living and life-giving force.
It is the special attribute
of the heart.

MAHATMA GANDHI
(1869-1948)

*W*e who lived in concentration
camps can remember the men
who walked through the huts
comforting others, giving away
their last piece of bread.
They may have been few in number,
but they offer sufficient proof
that everything can be taken away
from a man but one thing:
the last of the human freedoms –
to choose one's attitude
in any given set of circumstances,
to choose one's own way.

VIKTOR FRANKL

*S*o long as
little children
are allowed to suffer,
there is no true love
in this world.

ISADORA DUNCAN
(1878-1927)

*Without
the human community
one single human
being cannot survive.*

THE DALAI LAMA,
b. 1935

*L*OVE AND PITY
AND WISH WELL
TO EVERY SOUL
IN THE WORLD....

WILLIAM LAW
(1686-1761)

*P*ast the seeker as he prayed,
came the crippled and the beggar
and the beaten.
And seeing them, the holy one
went down into deep prayer
and cried, "Great God,
how is it that a loving creator
can see such things and yet do
nothing about them?"
And out of the long silence,
God said, "I did do something.
I made you."

SUFI TEACHING STORY

Love courses through everything,
No, Love <u>is</u> everything.
How can you say, <u>there is</u>
<u>no love</u>,
when nothing but Love exists?
All that you see has appeared
because of Love.
All shines from Love,
All pulses with Love,
All flows from Love –
No, once again all <u>is</u> Love!

FAKHRUDDIN ARAQI.
TRANSLATED BY
JONATHAN STAR

*T*he source of love
is deep in us
and we can help others
realize a lot of happiness.
One word, one action,
one thought can reduce
another person's suffering
and bring that person
joy.

THICH NHAT HANH

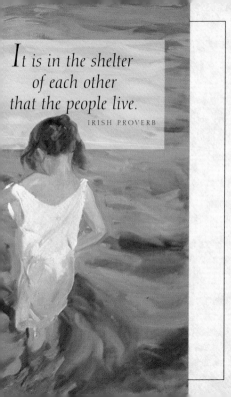

*It is in the shelter
of each other
that the people live.*

IRISH PROVERB

*L*ove is a choice
not simply, or necessarily,
a rational choice,

*but rather a willingness
to be present to others
without pretence or guile.*

CARTER HEYWARD

*When indeed shall we learn
that we are all related
one to the other,
that we are all members*

*of one body?
Until the spirit of love
for our fellow men,
regardless of race,*

color or creed,
shall fill the world,
making real in our lives
and our deeds the actuality
of human brotherhood –
until the great mass
of the people
shall be filled with
the sense of responsibility
for each other's welfare,
social justice
can never be attained.

HELEN KELLER
(1880-1968)

Be kind;
everyone you meet
is fighting a hard battle.

JOHN WATSON

It is not the perfect,
but the imperfect,
who have need of love.

OSCAR WILDE
(1854-1900)

So many people say
they want to save the world.
Just try your block,
will you?

REV. CECIL WILLIAMS

IT ISN'T WHAT YOU HAVE

IN YOUR POCKET

THAT'S IMPORTANT,

BUT WHAT YOU HAVE

IN YOUR HEART.

CARDINAL BERNADIN

The mother's battle
for her child —
with sickness, with poverty,
with war,
with all the forces
of exploitation
and callousness
that cheapen human life —
needs to become
a common human battle,
waged in love
and in the passion
for survival.

ADRIENNE RICH

*It doesn't matter how long
we may have been stuck
in a sense of our limitations.
If we go into a darkened room
and turn on the light,
it doesn't matter if the room
has been dark for a day,
or a week, or ten thousand years –
we turn on the light and it is
illumined. Once we contact our
capacity for love and happiness...
the light has been turned on.*

SHARON SALZBERG

... in the gentle relief
of another's care,
in the darkness
of night
and the winter's snow;
in the naked
and outcast –
seek love there.

WILLIAM BLAKE
(1757-1827)

*M*ay it be, oh Lord,
That I seek not so much
to be consoled as to console,
to be understood
as to understand,
to be loved as to love.
Because it is in giving oneself
that one receives;
it is in forgetting oneself
that one is found;
it is in pardoning
that one obtains pardon.

ST. FRANCIS OF ASSISI
(1181-1226)

*The cure for all
the ills and wrongs,
the cares, the sorrows
and crimes of
humanity, all lie in
that one word "love."
It is the divine vitality
that produces and
restores life.
To each and every one
of us it gives
the power of
working miracles,
if we will.*

LYDIA M CHILD

But my life, any life, real life, wasn't about pursuing the prizes of materialism and practising the gospel of self-gratification. Life was about enduring adversity, about being true to`oneself.... The real prizes were not... health, wealth and happiness, that facile trio which could be destroyed so easily by the first breath of misfortune, but faith, hope and, above all, love.

SUSAN HOWATCH

*Love always creates,
it never destroys.
In this lies man's
only promise.*

LEO BUSCAGLIA

*L*ove is something you and I
must have. We must have it
because our spirit feeds upon it.
We must have it because without it
we become weak and faint.
Without love
our self-esteem weakens.
Without it our courage fails.
Without love we can no longer
look confidently at the world.
We turn inward and begin to feed
upon our own personalities,

and little by little
we destroy it ourselves.
With it we are creative. With it
we march tirelessly.
With it and with it alone, we are
able to sacrifice for others.

CHIEF DAN GEORGE

*L*ove feels no burden, thinks nothing of trouble, attempts what is above its strength, pleads no excuse of impossibility.... It is therefore able to undertake all things, and it completes many things, and warrants them to take effect, where he who does not love would faint and lie down. Love is watchful and sleeping, slumbereth not. Though weary, it is not tired; though pressed, it is not straitened; though alarmed, it is not confounded....

THOMAS A. KEMPIS
(1379-1471)

*Loneliness
and the feeling
of being unwanted
is the most terrible
poverty.*

MOTHER TERESA, b.1910

This is the true joy of life,

the being used up for a purpose

recognized by yourself as a

mighty one; ... the being a force

of nature instead of a feverish

selfish little clod of ailments and

grievances, complaining

that the world will not devote

itself to making you happy.

I am of the opinion that my life

belongs to the community,

and as long as I live,

it is my privilege

to do for it what I can.

GEORGE BERNARD SHAW (1856–1950)

*L*ove is patient and kind;
love is not jealous, or conceited,
or proud; love is not ill-mannered,
or selfish, or irritable;
love does not keep a record
of wrongs: love is not happy
with evil, but is happy
with the truth.
Love never gives up: its faith,
hope and patience never fail.
Love is eternal....
There are faith, hope and love,
these three;
but the greatest of these is love.

1 CORINTHIANS 13:4

FOR FINALLY,
WE ARE AS WE LOVE.

IT IS LOVE THAT MEASURES
OUR STATURE.

WILLIAM SLOANE COFFIN

*L*ove seeketh not itself
to please
Nor for itself hath any care,
But for another gives its ease
And builds a heaven in hell's
despair.

WILLIAM BLAKE
(1757-1827)

*O*ne of the deepest
secrets of life
is that all that is really
worth doing
is what we do
for others.

LEWIS CARROLL
(1832-1898)

*T*o share often and much...
to know even one life has breathed
easier because you have lived.
This is to have succeeded

RALPH WALDO EMERSON
(1803-1882)

If I can stop one heart
from breaking,
I shall not live in vain;
If I can ease one life
the aching,
Or cool one pain
Or help one fainting robin
Unto his nest again,
I shall not live in vain.

EMILY DICKINSON
(1830-1886)

You will find as you look back
upon your life that the moments
when you have really lived
are the moments
when you have done things
in the spirit of love.

HENRY DRUMMOND
(1851-1897)

*We can do no great things – only
small things with great love.*

MOTHER TERESA.
b.1910

*I am done with great things
and big plans, great
institutions and big success.
I am for those tiny, invisible
loving human forces that
work from individual to
individual, creeping through
the crannies of the world like
so many rootlets, or like the
capillary oozing of water,
which, if given time, will
rend the hardest monuments
of pride.*

WILLIAM JAMES
(1842-1910)

*Each and every act of
kindness done by anyone
anywhere resonates out into
the world and somehow,
mysteriously, invisibly, and
perfectly, touches us all.*

THE EDITORS OF CONARI PRESS,
FROM
"RANDOM ACTS OF KINDNESS"

*W*e aspire to...
act with the eyes and heart
of compassion....
We know the happiness
of others in our
own happiness....
We know that every word,
every look, every action,
and every smile
can bring happiness
to others.

THICH NHAT HANH

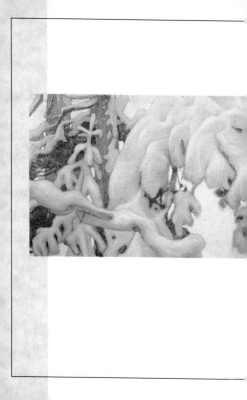

If we have no peace,
it is because
we have forgotten
that we belong
to each other.

MOTHER TERESA,
b.1910

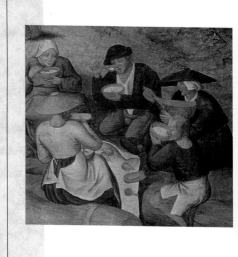

*I*n the end, nothing
we do or say
in this lifetime
will matter as much
as the way
we have loved
one another.

DAPHNE

ROSE

KINGMA

Acknowledgements: The publishers are grateful for permission to reproduce copyright material. Whilst every effort has been made to trace copyright holders, the publishers would be pleased to hear from any not here acknowledged. FAKHRUDDIN ARAQI: Extract from *Two Stars Rising* by Jonathan Star. Translation © 1991 by Jonathan Star. Published by Bantam Books, a division of Bantam Doubleday Dell Publishing Group, Inc. THICH NHAT HANH: Extract reprinted from *Teachings of Love* (1997) by Thich Nhat Hanh with permission of Parallax Press, Berkeley, California. DAPHNE ROSE KINGMA: Extract from *A Garland of Love* by Daphne Rose Kingma. Copyright 1992 © Daphne Rose Kingma. Published by Conari Press. SHARON SALZBERG: Extract from *The Practice of Kindness* by The Editors of Conari Press © 1996 by the Editors of Conari Press.

Picture Credits: Exley Publications would like to thank the following organizations and individuals for permission to reproduce their pictures. Whilst every effort has been made to trace copyright holders, the publishers would be pleased to hear from any not here acknowledged. Edimedia (EDI), Archiv für Kunst (AKG), The Bridgeman Art Library (BAL), Bulloz (BUL), Fine Art Photographic Library (FAP), Index (IND), ASIA, Superstock (SS). Cover and title page: Thomas Worsej, *Azaleas;* page 6: © 1997 Ernst Hassebrauk, *Music Lesson,* AKG; page 8: John George Sowerby, *The Box Seats,* BAL, page 10: Claude Monet, *Boulevard des Capucines;* page 12: John Atkinson